# HOT RODS

MOTOR Mania

by Eric Braun

Jan Lahtonen, consultant and safety engineer, auto mechanic, and lifelong automobile enthusiast

Lerner Publications Company • Minneapolis

Lerner Publications Company
A division of Lerner Publishing Group
241 First Avenue North
Minneapolis, MN 55401 U.S.A.

Website address: www.lernerbooks.com

Library of Congress Cataloging-in-Publication Data

Braun, Eric, 1971–
    Hot rods / by Eric Braun.
      p.   cm. — (Motor mania)
    Includes bibliographical references and index.
    ISBN-13: 978–0–8225–3531–7 (lib. bdg. : alk. paper)
    ISBN-10: 0–8225–3531–9 (lib. bdg. : alk. paper)
    1. Hot rods—Juvenile literature. 2. Automobiles—
Customizing—United States—Juvenile literature.
3. Popular culture—United States—Juvenile
literature. I. Title. II. Series.
    TL236.3.B725  2007
    629.228'6—dc22                2005019322

Manufactured in the United States of America
1 2 3 4 5 6 – DP – 12 11 10 09 08 07

# Contents

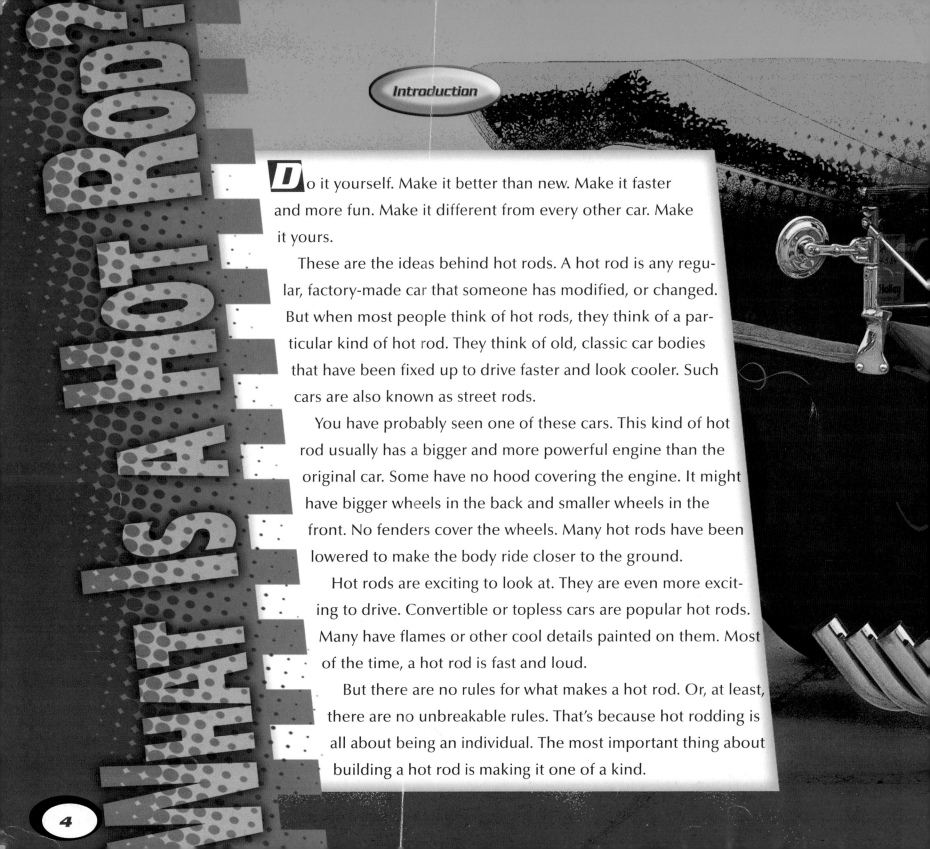

# WHAT IS A HOT ROD?

**D**o it yourself. Make it better than new. Make it faster and more fun. Make it different from every other car. Make it yours.

These are the ideas behind hot rods. A hot rod is any regular, factory-made car that someone has modified, or changed. But when most people think of hot rods, they think of a particular kind of hot rod. They think of old, classic car bodies that have been fixed up to drive faster and look cooler. Such cars are also known as street rods.

You have probably seen one of these cars. This kind of hot rod usually has a bigger and more powerful engine than the original car. Some have no hood covering the engine. It might have bigger wheels in the back and smaller wheels in the front. No fenders cover the wheels. Many hot rods have been lowered to make the body ride closer to the ground.

Hot rods are exciting to look at. They are even more exciting to drive. Convertible or topless cars are popular hot rods. Many have flames or other cool details painted on them. Most of the time, a hot rod is fast and loud.

But there are no rules for what makes a hot rod. Or, at least, there are no unbreakable rules. That's because hot rodding is all about being an individual. The most important thing about building a hot rod is making it one of a kind.

This hot rod was built for speed and looks. The black "T-Bucket" body is a classic hot rod style. This car has a large upgraded engine. The chrome (silver) box with the belt attached to the front is a supercharger. It boosts the car's power.

# Chapter One

# HOT ROD HISTORY

In 1908 Henry Ford *(below)* became famous for changing the world with his affordable and reliable car, the Model T Ford.

**C**ars first began appearing on streets in the late 1800s. But those first cars didn't work well, and they were expensive. Only wealthy people could afford them. Inventor Henry Ford changed all that in 1908. That year he introduced the Model T. This affordable and reliable car allowed millions of Americans to own cars for the first time. In the coming years, the Ford Model T gave millions of Americans the chance to enjoy the thrill of driving.

The 1920s, or the Roaring Twenties, were a great time for many Americans. Many were getting rich and having fun. Young people listened to thrilling jazz music. They packed theaters to see the world's first motion-picture movies. By this time, driving was another popular pastime. Cars had become a big part of growing up and recreation.

## The Great Depression

But in October 1929, everything changed. That's when the Great Depression began. The Great Depression was a time of poverty all over the world. Many businesses and banks closed. Millions of people lost their jobs and savings. Stores and factories had trouble selling anything. Most people had very little money to buy things. Some had no money at all.

The Great Depression hit every part of the United States. Many people lived in shacks. They couldn't afford to pay rent or make house payments. Thousands of people wandered the country in search of jobs.

During these hard years, it wasn't easy for a kid to find ways to have fun.

The Great Depression left millions of Americans homeless and out of work. Many left their homes and traveled the country in their Model T Fords in search of work.

But driving was still a fun pastime. Of course, new cars were too expensive for most teens. What could they do?

## Early Hot Rodding

In Southern California, young men began to find an answer. They bought used cars. Model Ts were popular because they didn't cost much. Drivers brought them to their own garages or backyards. There, they bent over the old machines and began to work.

Often these old cars didn't even run at first. But the young men quickly

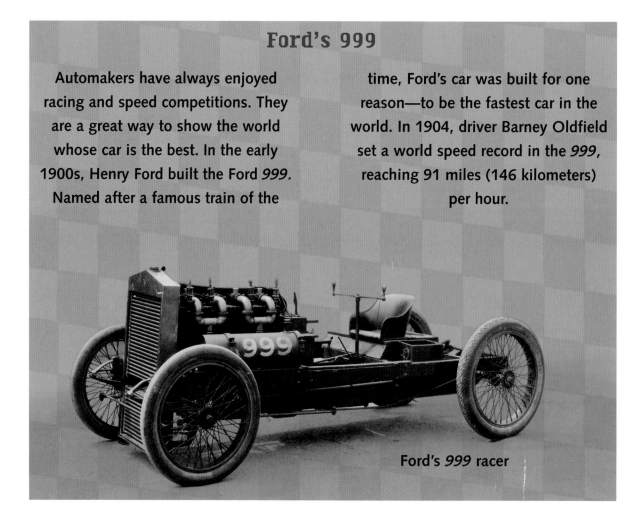

### Ford's 999

Automakers have always enjoyed racing and speed competitions. They are a great way to show the world whose car is the best. In the early 1900s, Henry Ford built the Ford *999*. Named after a famous train of the time, Ford's car was built for one reason—to be the fastest car in the world. In 1904, driver Barney Oldfield set a world speed record in the *999*, reaching 91 miles (146 kilometers) per hour.

Ford's *999* racer

1924 FORD MODEL T
(CIRCA 1948)
STREET ROADSTER

THIS EXAMPLE OF A BACKYARD-BUILT
ROADSTER IS TYPICAL OF THE TYPE
VEHICLE THAT BEGAN HOT RODDING.

IT IS ABSOLUTELY ORIGINAL AND AS IT
APPEARED ON THE JUNE 1948 COVER
OF HOT ROD MAGAZINE.

ENGINE:
1932 FORD V-8 WITH MAXI OVER-HEAD
EXHAUST VALVE CONVERSION

BEST PERFORMANCE:
120 MPH
(EL MIRAGE DRY LAKE - MAY 8, 1942)

BUILT AND OWNED SINCE 1938 BY:
ED ISKENDERIAN, GARDENA, CA

fixed that. They searched junkyards for free or cheap parts. They used their own time and labor. They learned about cars from the ground up. And once they had cars that ran, they hit the streets.

Hitting the streets usually meant racing. Back then, such competitions were rarely organized. Drivers raced each other whenever and wherever they could. Often they raced from one stoplight to the next on straight city streets.

As racing became more popular, the focus on speed grew. Drivers did anything they could to make their cars faster. Fords were perfect for this. They didn't weigh much, which made them faster. And many had a roadster body style. A roadster has no backseat, no top, and no side windows. This all made the car lighter and more

**This car is a classic 1924 Model T roadster hot rod. The owner has removed the fenders and hood to make it lighter.**

**HOT ROD TERM**
*Shave:* To remove the chrome, door handles, and badges to give a car a smoother look.

This classic roadster hot rod from the 1920s has some modern improvements. Note the arc-shaped roll bar behind the driver's seat. The roll bar protects the driver from being crushed if the car flips over.

streamlined. Roadsters cut through the air more easily.

Drivers removed the windshield, fenders, bumpers, and anything else they could. They installed smaller tires in front. These changes made their cars even lighter. Another common change was to lower the car so it rode close to the ground. A road-hugging car turns better at high speeds. In the back, bigger tires were added to increase traction. These changes gave the car a forward tilt called a rake.

Of course, the drivers also "souped up" their cars for high performance. For example, many drivers replaced their cars' old engines with bigger, more powerful engines. In 1932, Ford came out with an engine known as the Flathead V8. (A V8 is an engine with eight cylinders arranged in the shape of a V.) The Flathead V8 was much more powerful than the 4-cylinder engines in earlier cars. When drivers matched this big engine with a small, lightweight body, they ended up with a very fast car.

# How an Internal Combustion Engine Works

Almost all hot rods have internal combustion V8 engines. Some hot rodders have big, modern engines in their cars. Others prefer old, classic engines like the Flathead Ford V8. Like most car engines, they run on gasoline and use a four stroke cycle. The four stroke cycle burns a mixture of air and gas to power the car. These cycles take place thousands of times per minute inside a car engine.

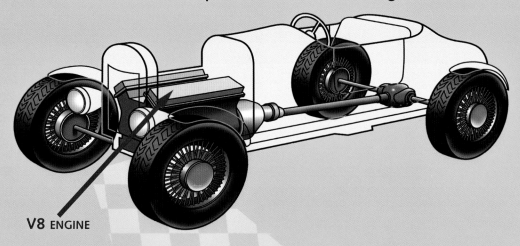

V8 ENGINE

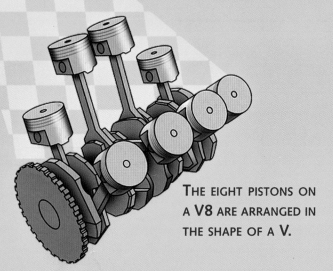

THE EIGHT PISTONS ON A V8 ARE ARRANGED IN THE SHAPE OF A V.

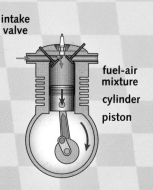

intake valve
fuel-air mixture
cylinder
piston

**1. INTAKE STROKE**
The piston moves down the cylinder and draws the fuel-air mixture into the cylinder through the intake valve.

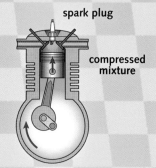

spark plug
compressed mixture

**2. COMPRESSION STROKE**
The piston moves up and compresses the fuel-air mixture. The spark plug ignites the mixture, creating combustion (burning).

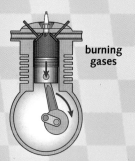

burning gases

**3. POWER STROKE**
The burning gases created by combustion push the piston downward. This gives the engine its power.

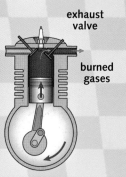

exhaust valve
burned gases

**4. EXHAUST STROKE**
The piston moves up again and pushes out the burned-out exhaust gases through the exhaust valve.

Personalized license plates—called vanity plates—are a popular accessory on hot rods. Note the two pipes on the back of this car. This is a sign the car has dual high-performance headers (exhaust pipes).

Other ways to soup up a car included adding straight, loud exhaust pipes. The pipes increase power by letting the engine breathe more easily. The result was a fast, noisy, machine.

Besides speed, uniqueness was important. No two hot rods were exactly the same. Drivers were proud of this. They didn't have factory-made cars that had thousands of copies. Instead, they each built a one-of-a-kind hot rod.

## Dry Lake Racing

Street racing could only go so far. It was dangerous and illegal. Soon drivers discovered that dry lake beds were a great place to race. The most famous of these was Lake Muroc, which is northeast of Los Angeles, California. These dry lake beds are flat, smooth, and hard. They're perfect for running a car as fast as it can go.

Dry lake racing became very popular

### Lake Muroc

The first organized racing event at Lake Muroc, California, took place on March 25, 1931. Many more races followed in the next few years. Cars often topped speeds of 100 miles (161 km) per hour. The excitement ended during the spring of 1938. The U.S. Army Air Forces owned the land in the area and sent in troops to break up the events. Hot rodders were forced to test their vehicles on different dry lake beds. But racing returned to Lake Muroc in 1995.

in the 1930s. But the races were crowded, unorganized, and dangerous. Sometimes 20 or more cars raced at once. Each car raised huge plumes of dust and dirt. If a driver fell behind the pack, he couldn't see anything. Ugly accidents often resulted, and drivers were sometimes injured or killed.

People outside this racing culture didn't understand it. They heard about the accidents. They saw and heard the dangerous, noisy street racing and the sometimes strange-looking cars. They saw the car clubs with names such as the Outriders and the Sidewinders. The clubs gained a reputation for being outlaws and troublemakers.

In 1937, a man named Art Tilton organized the Southern California Timing Association (SCTA). Its

## Hot Rodding Mechanics

U.S. Navy mechanics *(left)* work on the engine of an aircraft during World War II (1939–1945). During the war, many hot rodders served in the military as mechanics. Their skill with engines was valuable to the war effort. At the same time, the mechanics learned a lot from their experiences working on high-tech airplane engines. Mechanics who worked on them learned many tricks about how to get the best performance out of their planes. After the war, these same men brought their skills back to the hot rodding world.

purpose was to supervise dry lake racing and to improve the image of car racers. Many clubs joined the SCTA. This unique driving culture was becoming more organized.

### World War II

Things changed at the end of the 1930s. World War II began in 1939. The United States joined the war near the end of 1941. Even before the United States got into the war, Lake Muroc was made into a base for the U.S. Army Air Forces. This took away one of the best lakes for racing. Still, many racers ended up back at Lake Muroc. This time, they were in the air force. With their skill for working on car engines, they also made great airplane mechanics.

Many other racers became soldiers. They were shipped out to fight all over the world. While in the service, they shared stories about their cars and the good times they had fixing them up and driving them. This helped to spread the word about this exciting hobby. After the war ended in 1945, non-Californians everywhere began to work on cars in their own backyards. The trend spread throughout the United States.

### The Postwar Years

In the years after the war, Americans got back on their feet. Jobs were created and people had money to spend. The Great Depression was over.

During this time, a new nickname for these special kind of cars popped up—hot rods. People who worked on and drove these cars became known as hot rodders.

Meanwhile, young drivers had more money to spend on their cars. Many drivers could afford to give their rods an eye-catching paint job and new upholstery. A lot of people could afford to buy new cars. Many people customized, or changed, their new cars more for looks than for racing. They added chrome to their engines, whitewall tires, swooping fender skirts (metal covers over the wheels), and other fancy details. These became known as custom cars. Traditional hot rodders looked down on the new trend. They felt true hot rodding was about speed, not looks.

**HOT ROD TERM**
*Speed shop:* a place that sells high-performance car parts

Historically, hot rodders *(left)* have loved speed. But lack of simple safety features on early hot rods—such as seat belts—meant that accidents were often deadly.

## Bonneville Salt Flats

Meanwhile, during the late 1940s, drivers were still racing in the dry lakes of Southern California. The most popular lake was El Mirage. But the racing course at this lake was only 1.3 miles (2.1 km) long. This was too short a distance for some cars to get up to full speed. Without access to the biggest and best lake, Muroc, dry lake racing was not the same.

So the SCTA began to look for a new spot to race. The racers found the Bonneville Salt Flats in Utah. A salt flat is the bed of a dried-up saltwater lake. These spots have a hard, flat surface that is perfect for racing. The Bonneville Salt Flats are nearly 90 miles (145 km) long, so there was plenty of room to set up a racing course. Drivers could go as fast as they wanted on the hard, flat salt.

At this time, the SCTA was the country's leading hot rodding organization. In 1948 the association's first elected president, Wally Parks, went to Salt Lake City, Utah, to get permission to race in the salt flats.

City officials didn't like the idea at first. Hot rodders still had a bad reputation. But finally, Parks and his partners convinced them. In August 1949, the SCTA had its first Bonneville Speed Week in the Bonneville Salt Flats. About 60 cars participated.

A hot rodder makes some final adjustments to his car before a race.

## Wally Parks

Wally Parks *(right)* has been involved in the SCTA from the start. He also served as the first editor for *Hot Rod* magazine and helped found the National Hot Rod Association (NHRA). Through the association and the magazine, Parks worked to make hot rodding a big-time sport. In 1998, the Wally Parks NHRA Motor Sports Museum opened in Pomona, California.

For safety reasons, the SCTA changed how it handled racing events. At previous events, dozens of cars raced at the same time. The roaring vehicles kicked up dust, making it impossible for drivers to see if they had fallen behind. To solve this problem, the SCTA introduced a time trial system. Instead of racing in a pack to see who was fastest, each driver took his turn running the course alone. Each run was timed, and the fastest time earned first prize. The time trial system allowed drivers to push their cars to the limit without fear of hitting other cars. Drivers experienced the thrill of high-speed driving with less risk of injury or death.

The first organized event at the Bonneville Salt Flats was a big success.

## A Name That Sells

One American automaker decided to use the Bonneville Salt Flats craze to sell its new model of car. In 1957, Pontiac named its new car line the Bonneville.

A hot rod breaks into pieces after an accident at the Bonneville Salt Flats in 1953. Although the time trial system was safer than multicar races, high-speed driving could still be deadly.

The fastest car reached an amazing speed of 193 miles (311 km) per hour. Best of all, everyone had fun and no one was hurt. The SCTA decided to hold more events there in the coming years. The Bonneville time trials have become a hot rodding tradition.

## The Golden Age of Hot Rodding

Meanwhile, hot rodders had found new ways to share and learn more about their sport. *Hot Rod* magazine began publishing two years before the first Bonneville time trials. *Hot Rod* was the first magazine dedicated to hot rodding. It had more than 300,000 readers by 1950. Hot rodding was becoming huge.

Legal drag strips began to open up, too. Drag strips are paved, straight racetracks where cars can really fly. Most strips have two separate lanes where two cars can line up and race to the finish. The first strip was set up at an airport in Southern California in 1950. Before then, drag racing had been going on for years in the streets. But this was both dangerous and illegal. At drag strips, two racers could compete safely without worrying about getting the cops on their tails.

## Drag Racing and Street Rods

Drag racing became a professional sport in 1953. That was the year the NHRA held its first race. Soon the sport grew in popularity as the NHRA held drag racing competitions around the country. And so the term *hot rod* started to mean many different things, including drag racing and customizing. But traditional hot rodding has always been about driving in the streets. This led to a new term— *street rods.* Many people give the name street rods to traditional hot rods driven on public roads.

Two cars tear up the track at the start of a drag race in California in 1957.

19

With racing getting more and more popular, hot rodders needed high-performance parts for their souped-up vehicles. It was not enough to hunt through a junkyard. Some parts couldn't be found anywhere—because they didn't exist. In the 1950s, some hot rodders began to make and sell the new parts themselves.

Most people think of the 1950s as the golden age of hot rodding. Cars were a huge part of life for young people. Young drivers hung out at malt shops and drive-ins, showing off their cars. Cruising—just driving around from one hangout to the next—was the most popular pastime for millions of young Americans. Local car clubs sprang up all over. Many clubs staged car shows, where hot rodders could compare cars, share ideas, and hang out with other hot rodders.

## 1960s to Modern Times

The hot rodding craze lost some steam in the 1960s. One reason was that customizing and hot rods had gotten so fancy. Drivers put so much time and money into making the perfect car that they didn't want to drive them. They worried the cars would get damaged! Many people began to leave their prized possessions in their garages. They forgot why hot rodding had been fun—driving.

Another reason was that automakers were making powerful cars that didn't have to be souped up. In the early 1960s, the three big U.S. automakers—General Motors, Ford, and

Chrysler—were building "muscle cars." These were like ready-made hot rods. They were fast, with powerful (or "muscular") engines and slick styling. Many people say the 1964 Pontiac GTO was the first true muscle car. It was a medium-sized car with a big, powerful engine. Later came other, similar muscle cars, such as the Plymouth Road Runner, the Dodge Challenger, the Oldsmobile 4-4-2, the Chevrolet Chevelle SS, the Ford Mustang Cobra, and many more.

But hot rodding didn't stay down for long. In the 1970s, it began to roar back. Hot rodders from previous years were still interested in fixing up old cars. And these older hot rodders had more money to spend on their cars. Meanwhile, a new generation of fans was growing up. Hot rod shows drew huge crowds around the country. Hot rodders young and old formed new car clubs.

The rebirth of hot rodding continued through the 1980s and 1990s. In modern times, it is as popular as ever. Hot rodders can enjoy their hobby by reading hot rod magazines, visiting auto shows, and watching shows about cars and hot rods on television. And they can buy parts from dozens of custom parts makers. Hot rodders can even have highly-skilled mechanics soup-up their cars for them at customizing garages. All this has turned hot rodding into a multimillion-dollar business. What once was a way for young drivers with little money to have fun has become a permanent part of American culture.

**HOT ROD TERM**
**Hi-boy:** A Ford roadster or coupe that has not been channeled to make it sit lower

This 1930s Ford coupe has a powerful modern engine and "suicide doors" (doors hinged at the back). Suicide doors got their name because they can be easy to fall out of.

# Chapter Two

# HOT ROD CULTURE

Hot rodders take their classic Model T rod for a spin *(below)*. For most hot rodders, the thrill of driving is still the best part of their hobby.

In the first years of hot rodding, the pastime wasn't very organized. This was during the early years of the Great Depression of the 1930s. Some hot rodders formed small clubs and timing associations. But drivers probably didn't think of hot rodding as an organized sport. And they rarely thought about safety. Mostly, they just wanted to have fun.

Early hot rodders didn't worry about their image, either. They didn't care what other people thought about them. However, most people thought they were dangerous troublemakers.

But as years passed, hot rodding grew in popularity. Some hot rodders began to think about safety and image.

Police officers were giving hot rodders a hard time. And drivers were getting killed in accidents. By the late 1930s, it was time to start changing things.

## The SCTA, the NHRA, and the NSRA

In 1937, the SCTA became the first big organization of hot rodders. The group started to enforce rules for safety. It also began to work on giving hot rodders a better image. SCTA officers met with local government officials and with groups like the National Safety Council and the Parent Teacher Association. The purpose of these meetings was always to spread a good image for hot rodders. SCTA officials also convinced local community leaders to allow organized legal races.

Car shows—featuring many kinds of custom cars—are a great way for hot rod owners to show off their machines.

Since street racing is illegal, police and hot rodders have often been in conflict. But groups like the SCTA helped organize the sport. They found places where hot rodders could race legally. The sport now has a better reputation.

The SCTA also organized hot rod shows, where the fastest and best-looking hot rods could be seen. There, the public got to see the good side of hot rodding. This improved hot rodding's image and drew more people into the hobby. In the twenty-first century, the SCTA still organizes races at the Bonneville Salt Flats in Utah and

## Hot Rod Clubs

Hot rod clubs have existed almost from the beginning of hot rodding. Some have joined the SCTA over the years. The first clubs to join the SCTA were the Sidewinders, the Idlers, the Ramblers, the Throttlers, the Road Runners, and the Night Riders.

California's El Mirage lake bed.

The NHRA is another important hot rodding organization. The NHRA formed in the 1950s. It organizes most of the legal drag races in the United States. It was created as a way for hot rodders to race on drag strips instead of public roads. Back then, the organization's slogan was, "Off the street and on the strip."

The NHRA hosted its first race in 1953 in Pomona, California. In 1955, it hosted its first national event, called the Nationals. It took place in Great Bend, Kansas. The competition became a yearly event that draws

## Drag Racing

A drag race begins as black smoke shoots out of the headers of this hot rod's Ford Flathead V8 engine. Drag racing is a popular sport across the United States.

tens of thousands of fans. The NHRA has grown steadily over the years. It organized more than 5,000 events in 2005 and is the world's largest motorsports organization. It has more than 80,000 members.

The National Street Rod Association (NSRA) is a more traditional organization. The NSRA is for hot rodders who prefer to drive their modified cars on the street, the way the first hot rodders did. It was founded in 1970 and hosts 11 non-racing events a year, including the Street Rod Nationals. The events are aimed at families and include trade shows, where people sell parts and cars. The NSRA defines a street rod as any vehicle from 1948 or earlier that has been modified to meet the driver's needs.

The NSRA focuses on creativity, not speed. The organization produces a monthly magazine called *StreetScene*. It includes features on the coolest street rods, street rod events, and much more.

## Hot Rod Magazines

The most famous hot rodding magazine is *Hot Rod*. It launched in 1948 as the first publication created just for hot rodders. *Hot Rod's* founders carried issues of their magazine around in their cars. They sold them at races and other events. The publications caught on very quickly. The spread of *Hot Rod* magazine helped hot rodding catch on all over the country. It is still an important resource for hundreds of thousands of hot rodders everywhere.

A parade of hot rods cruises across the dry salt flats at Bonneville, Utah. Hot rodders show off their creativity at hot rod events such as this one.

HRM TESTS 8-WHEELED "MOUNTAIN GOAT" JEEP

HOT ROD
MAGAZINE

MAY 1952 25c
OVER HALF-MILLION COPIES
THIS ISSUE

This auto show display brings
to life one of the most
famous *Hot Rod* magazine
covers, from May 1952.
The car is a customized
1929 Ford roadster.

Hot rodding pioneers Robert "Pete" Petersen *(left)* and Wally Parks *(right)* at the Bonneville Salt Flats. The two men were key figures in bringing racing to Bonneville.

*Hot Rod* covers car-related events all over the world. It also gives instructions for projects, profiles cars and trends, and more. Other important hot rodding magazines include *Street Rodder, Car Craft,* and *Rod & Custom*. Like *Hot Rod*, these magazines help hot rodders stay up-to-date with the latest events and trends.

## Hot Rod Movies

The post-World War II hot rod craze was the subject of many "B" movies of the 1950s and 1960s. Films such as *Hot Rod Girl* (1956), *Dragstrip Riot* (1958), and *Speed Crazy* (1959) weren't very well done and didn't star well-known actors. But they were fun, and featured cool cars, pretty women, tough guys, and exciting races.

## Car Museums

The International Motorsports Hall of Fame and Museum is in Talladega, Alabama. It lies next to the world-famous Talladega Superspeedway, the fastest racetrack in the world. The museum includes more than 100 vehicles that have been important to the history of motorsports. The museum houses a Motorsports Hall of Fame for the most important drivers, engineers, builders, and leaders of motorsports history. Wally Parks became a member in 1992.

The Wally Parks NHRA Motorsports Museum is in Pomona, California. This museum houses vehicles, artifacts, and stories that tell the history of fast and stylish cars. It focuses on hot rods, customs, race cars, and speed records. It also focuses on Southern California's role as the historic center for the cars' past and present development.

## Custom Garages and Speed Shops

These days, not all hot rodders do it themselves. Custom garages have become a big business. These shops build custom machines for people who want hot rods but don't have the time or the knowledge to build their own.

**This deuce roadster is a real work of art. It has a gleaming paint job with flames and a modern engine with lots of chrome. The small metal tank on the front is probably a gas tank.**

A close-up of this spotless engine shows the hard work and detail that goes into a hot rod project.

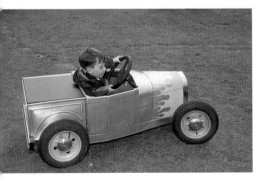

A young hot rodder-to-be tries out his own little custom car.

People who still enjoy working on cars can visit speed shops. These auto stores sell high-performance equipment for hot rods. The

### Chop Job

A popular way to customize a hot rod is to "chop" it. Chopping a car means cutting off the roof (or other part) and attaching it at a lower height. The result is a shorter car that cuts through the air more easily.

stores are also good places to meet other hot rodders.

In the 2000s, hot rodding remains as popular as ever. A big part of the fun is hanging out at hot rodding events. Car shows and rod runs are held just for this purpose. Hot rodders get together to show off their rides, swap stories, share secrets, and drive hot rods. These events usually feature activities for kids, live bands, and hot rod judging. Shows are sponsored by the SCTA, the NHRA, and the NSRA, as well as many local clubs and groups.

The Americruise is a yearly event sponsored by *Rod & Custom*. In the Americruise, hot rodders tour the country together. Drivers can sign up and drop in at any stop along the way. Hot rodders all get together at the end for a big show and a party. It's a great way for hot rodders to build a strong community.

A pack of hot rods cruise along the salt flats of Bonneville.

# Building a Hot Rod

Taking a beat up old car and making it new is a big challenge. It takes a lot of time, skill—and money. But for many people, it is a true labor of love. Ron Herrmann of Andover, Minnesota, has restored several cars and made them into hot rods over the years. Here are a few steps in the process Ron used to restore an old 1938 Chevy coupe into a work of art.

**1.** The old 1938 Chevy wasn't looking too good when Ron purchased it. It had been sitting outdoors for years and was rusting. Ron had his work cut out for him.

**3.** The body is primed—given a coat of special paint that sticks to the metal—and then sanded to remove any bumps. Dents are filled with a special compound and then sanded for smoothness. Once the body has been made flawless, it is primed again.

**2.** One of the first jobs for any restoration is to remove the body and the engine from the frame. (The frame is the part of the car that the engine and the body are attached to.) Here Ron has stripped the car down to the frame and added some additional pieces for extra strength.

**4.** The car is beginning to come together. The hood, cowl (front end), and fender are bolted on to make sure they fit correctly. They will be removed again for painting.

**5.** Ron has chosen a lightning bolt paint scheme for the car. White lightning bolt detailing shoots across the hood of the car. The lightning bolts will show clearly with the final paint job.

**6.** The finished product is a jaw-dropping purple Chevy coupe with lightning bolts and chrome wheels. A pile of junk has been turned into a work of art.

## Ford Model T

This is an original Ford Model T. First introduced in 1908, these cars were built to be affordable and reliable. They were not built for speed. A Model T fresh from the factory had a top speed of about 45 miles (72 km) per hour.

## Ford Model T "T-Bucket"

This is one of the most famous hot rods of all time. Twenty-two-year-old hot rodder Norm Grabowski built this T-Bucket in the 1950s using a Ford Model T body and parts from many different cars. Grabowski's machine, which got its nickname from the open-air bucket-like shape of the passenger compartment, appeared on the cover of the October 1955 issue of *Hot Rod*. The car started a whole new trend toward "bucket" hot rods.

## Ford T-Bucket Hot Rod

This is a classic T-Bucket hot rod, built for looks and speed. The builder has added chrome to nearly every visible part. The fat rear tires give the car a ton of traction at the drag strip. Check out the large oval shaped roll bar behind the passenger compartment.

## Ford Model T Roadster Hot Rod

The rounded trunk of this car shows it to be a Model T roadster. But this car is clearly a one-of-a-kind. Wide tires and an orange flaming paint job make this car a standout. Chrome engine parts, steering wheel, dashboard, exhaust, and wheels give it a flawless look. Other details include "deep dish" wheel rims and eight chrome air intakes on the top of the engine.

## Ford Model T Pickup Hot Rod

If one V8 engine can make a car fast, how about two? The builder of this hot rod has created a truly wild ride. The car's body is probably from a fiberglass kit, instead of an original steel Model T body. The builder has stretched out the frame and bolted on a pair of modern V8 engines. The headers are known as four-into-ones, because the four separate pipes combine into one collector pipe.

## 1932 Ford Model A Hot Rod

Ford produced the Model T for nearly 20 years. It was replaced in 1928 by the Model A. In later years, the sturdy and reliable machine became a hit with hot rodders. This Model A has been given a basic hot rod treatment. The Ford Flathead V8 engine features chrome speed parts. Red wheel rims and white sidewall tires complete the classic look.

## 1932 Ford Model A Street Rod

This Model A has been modified for both looks and speed. The fenders and bumpers have been removed. The Flathead V8 engine is packed with speed parts. The short header exhaust pipes show that this car has no muffler, making the car very loud. The front end has been lowered to give the car a rake. Note the checkered-flag racing themes, including the badge on the side. The firewall (the wall between the engine and passenger compartments) is also checkered.

## 1934 Ford Roadster

This 1934 Ford roadster has been customized in typical hot rod fashion. The modern V8 engine sports numerous chrome parts. The car has not been channeled, or lowered. This original setup is known as a hi-boy. Fat rear wheels and whitewall tires are other classic features. The pull-out rear seat is known as a "rumble seat."

## 1932 Ford Roadster "Woody"

This classic deuce roadster has a rare feature—wood body panels. Wood bodied cars—often known as woodies—were trendy in the 1930s and 1940s. Some people liked the look of them. But these cars were never huge sellers. Part of the reason is that the wood is very hard to keep looking new.

## Ford Model A Roadster

These hot rodders are reliving the past with this simple roadster hot rod. Many of the features seen on this car are typical of hot rods of the 1940s and 1950s. They include a basic gray paint job, whitewall tires, Mobilgas badge, and simple black rims. These hot rodders are even dressed for the part. Note their 1950s jackets and hats.

## ord Roadster Hot Rod

This hot rod is a customized version of an early 1930s Ford roadster. Unlike many hot rods, this car still sports a hood. This leaves room for an exciting flaming paint job. The car also has "knock-off rims." The spiked center piece on the rims is designed to be spun off with the knock of a hammer for fast wheel changes during races.

## 1933 Ford Roadster

The builder of this machine has done some extreme customizing. The gleaming flame paint job is just one of many wild details on this 1933 roadster. This car features a modern V8--instead of a Flathead Ford— engine with chrome plated parts. The supercharged engine is topped with a large air intake, which sucks in lots of air for added power.

## Custom Roadster Hot Rod

The creator of this machine has taken the low, smooth look to an extreme. The grille in front has been customized to slope upward from the bottom. The windshield has been chopped and the door handles have been shaved. Even the rearview mirrors on the side have been shrunk. The car has no bumpers, fenders, or running board (the shelf beneath the door that people step on to get inside the car). An eye-popping orange paint job completes the look.

### *Flash Fighter*

This car was built by a Swedish hot rodder, Ove Skoog. The body is a 1934 Ford "three-window" (two side windows and a rear window) coupe. The car's unique nose design was built to look like a fighter plane. During World War II, many U.S. fighter planes featured similar shark-toothed grins. The bullet-shaped cone coming out of the grille takes this look to a new level. Skoog named his car *Flash Fighter*.

## "Drop Tank" Lakester

This is an example of a car built strictly for racing on the salt flats. Its teardrop-shaped body once served as an underwing fuel tank on a World War II aircraft. (Aircraft often carried such tanks beneath their wings on long missions. They are called drop tanks because the pilots dropped the tanks when they were empty.) These cars were built to be light and very fast.

## 1933 Ford Coupe

This 1933 Ford three-window coupe dominated the salt flats in the early 1950s. The car continued to race into the 1990s, reaching speeds of well over 220 miles (354 km) per hour. The car's roof has been chopped very low to make it as streamlined as possible. Check out the suicide doors.

## Chopped and Shaved Olds

This late 1930s or early 1940s Olds (Oldsmobile) sedan has been customized for a smooth look. The roof has been chopped. The headlights, taillights, and front grille have been "frenched." They are set inside the fenders.

## Chopped and Shaved Olds

The raised slits on the trunk and the hood of this Olds sedan are known as louvers. Louvers were a common feature on the hoods of very early cars. They allowed air into the engine compartment to help keep the engine cool. These louvers were probably added to this car for looks more than anything else. The small, snakelike bumpers are known as "nerf bars."

## Ford Hot Rod Custom

This custom car is based on the design of a Ford coupe from the late 1930s. The creator of this car was aiming for a smooth look. Note how the fenders are molded—not bolted—to the body. The teardrop front fenders, sleek grille, chopped roof, and ultra-thin hood add to the sculpted look. The chrome lines of the front grille have been stretched to reach the doors and fenders, and the door handles have been shaved.

## Mercury "Lead Sled"

This car is a heavily customized late 1940s or early 1950s Mercury. It has been modified to give it a "lead sled" look. The big, roomy body has been smoothed out to make the car look as sleek as possible. The roof has been chopped. Fender skirts cover the back wheels. The result is a car that looks big, heavy, and low. The colorful paint job with vivid stripes is a popular style on this kind of car.

## "Suede" 1950 Ford

Ford sold more than one million of these simple, snazzy cars in the late 1940s and early 1950s. Many hot rodders like their classic shape. The car's simple look is a style from the old hot rodding days. The flat (not shiny) black paint is actually primer. Because they couldn't afford to prime and paint their cars at the same time, some hot rodders drove their cars around with just the primer. A few liked the look so much they decided to leave them that way.

## *The Emperor*

This one-of-a-kind car was built by famous customizer George Barris. Barris has been making incredible cars since the 1940s. He is best known for the many famous cars he built for television shows and movies, including the Batmobile from the 1960s *Batman* TV series. Built in the late 1950s, *The Emperor* is a 1929 Ford roadster with chromefrom front to back. The front grill is like no other. The six "pipes" on top of the engine are air intakes.

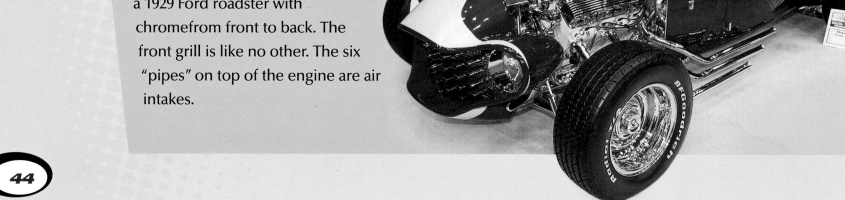

## The Invader

This car is another George Barris creation. The *Invader*'s look features a wild spaceship-like body and two big V8 engines mounted side by side. Barris's other cars include the *Munsters Koach* from the 1960s show *The Munsters* and the *General Lee* from the 1980s show *The Dukes of Hazzard*.

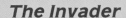

## Manta Ray

This famous one-of-a-kind machine was created by car builder Dean Jeffries in the early 1960s. The custom-built body was attached to the frame of an Italian Maserati sports car. The Plexiglass canopy (windshield) looks like the kind found on jet fighters.

# Glossary

**chop:** to lower or shorten a car part (often the roof) by cutting some of it away and attaching it at a lower height

**custom:** a vehicle that has been modified for its looks more than for driving. It is often spelled *kustom*.

**drag racing:** a race in a straight line. Drag racing originally was done on city streets but later became a professional sport. NHRA drag racing is done mostly on a drag strip that is ¼ mile (.4 km) long.

**fender:** a metal covering over the wheel of a car

**rake:** the forward tilt a hot rod gets after large tires are added to the back and small ones are added to the front

**roadster:** a two-seat car with no top and no side windows

**skirts:** metal covers that attach to the rear fenders of a car and cover the wheels. Skirts are popular on customs.

**streamlined:** designed or changed to move through the air quickly and easily

**street rod:** a hot rod that is made for the street. This term came into use when hot rodders wanted a word to describe these traditional hot rods as compared to the many hot rods that were being used for drag racing.

## Selected Bibliography

Baskerville, Gray. "The Rise and Haul of Hot Rodding." Hot Rod magazine. N.d. http://www.hotrod.com/thehistoryof/42646 (December 14, 2004).

Bertilsson, Bo. *Classic Hot Rods*. Osceola, WI: MBI Publishing, 1999.

*50 Years of Hot Rod: From the Editors of* Hot Rod *Magazine*. Osceola, WI: MBI Publishing, 1998.

Ganahl, Pat. *Hot Rods and Cool Customs*. New York: Abbeville Press, 1996.

Medley, Tom. *Tex Smith's Hot Rod History: Book One: The Beginnings*. Driggs, ID: Tex Smith Publishing, 1994.

———. *Stock Cars*. Minneapolis: Lerner Publications Company, 2007.

*Hot Rod* magazine. Los Angeles: Primedia, monthly.

## Further Reading

Benford, Tom. *Street Rod*. Saint Paul: Motorbooks International, 2004.

Doeden, Matt. *Lowriders*. Minneapolis: Lerner Publications Company, 2007.

## Websites

*International Motorsports Hall of Fame and Museum*
http://www.motorsportshalloffame.com
Learn about famous hot rodders and other car drivers.

*Official Site of the National Hot Rod Association*
http://www.nhra.com
Find out more about drag racing events, drivers, and more.

*Wally Parks NHRA Motorsports Museum*
http://museum.nhra.com
Cruise through the photo gallery, read the latest news on the NHRA, and more.

# Index

## About the Author
Eric Braun has written and edited dozens of books for children on a wide variety of topics. Among the books he has written are *Tony Hawk*, *Norway in Pictures*, *Canada in Pictures*, and *Uganda in Pictures*. He lives in Minneapolis, Minnesota, with his wife and two sons.

## About the Consultant
Jan Lahtonen is a safety engineer, auto mechanic, and lifelong automobile enthusiast.

## Photo Acknowledgments
The images in this book are used with the permission of: © Mike Key, pp. 4–5, 9, 10, 21, 22 (bottom), 25, 27, 29, 30 (all), 34 (bottom), 35 (all), 36 (all), 37 (all), 38 (all), 39 (all), 40 (all), 41 (all), 42 (all), 43 (all), 44 (all), 45 (all); © Hulton Archive/Getty Images, pp. 6 (top), 8; Library of Congress, p. 6 (bottom) (LC-USZ62-096679); © Charles E. Steinheimer/Time Life Pictures/Getty Images, p. 7; © Wayne Zuehlke, pp. 12, 23; © Historic Photo Archive/Hulton Archive/ Getty Images, p. 13; National Archives, p. 14; Ralph Crane/Time Life Pictures/Getty Images, pp. 15, 19, 20, 24; © J.R. Eyerman/ Time Life Pictures/Getty Images, pp. 16, 18; © Allan Grant/Time Life Pictures/Getty Images, p. 17; © Landspeed Productions, Inc., p. 22 (top), 26, 28, 31; © Ron Herrmann/Rich Linngren, pp. 32 (all), 33 (all); © Ed Clark/Time Life Pictures/Getty Images, p. 34 (top).

Front Cover: © PhotoEquity/Artemis Images.